GAY SCIE

by the same author

The Turn of the Cucumber

GAY SCIENCE
ANN DRYSDALE

PETERLOO POETS

First published in 1999
by Peterloo Poets
2 Kelly Gardens, Calstock, Cornwall PL18 9SA, U.K.

**A catalogue record for this book is available
from the British Library**

ISBN 1-871471-76-1

Printed in Great Britain by
Antony Rowe Ltd, Chippenham, Wilts.

ACKNOWLEDGEMENTS:

"Gay Science" and "The Stainless Child" first appeared in *Of Sawn Grain* (The Collective Press)

"Language Difficulty" first appeared in *Poetry Wales* and is included in *20th Century Anglo-Welsh Poetry* edited by Dannie Abse (Seren) "Small Farm at the Edge of Town" first appeared in New Welsh Review.

"The Painter's Mother" first appeared in *Prop*.

"Rupert" won second prize in the 1996 Manchester Poetry Competition.

"What Janet Said" won the Dylan Thomas Prize and *Poetry Digest*'s 1994 United Kingdom Bard of the Year Award.

For Philip Gray

Has tibi symphonias pletrat sophus, induperator.
Alcuin (to Charlemagne)

Contents

Gay Science *

There are as many languages as there are people
(Not 'peoples', Editor; it's not that easy)
And words mean only what we believe them to mean.

My poem is an invisible sketch in the space between us
Of what I believe my words mean. Giving it to you
Hands you carte blanche on which to draw
Invisibly what you have understood.

You show me yours; I show you mine:
It gets neither of us anywhere yet
We are both the richer for it.

Sometimes I can almost convince myself
That if you boil prose till the thin liquor evaporates
And agitate what's left till the words spin,
What settles-out is poetry.

But instinct tells me it lies at the interface
Between what I know and you believe
And may slip between them without touching.

We are no nearer a definition.
Distillations of the very essence of something.
Short-circuits jumping the gaps between minds.

Synopses; synapses. Whatever.
You could call it like calling to like
If you like.

* *"Gay science" — a rendering of "gai saber"*
   the Provençal name for the art of poetry.

South Wales, Singing

Should you be seeking the sound of South Wales
It will save time to exclude false promises
Held out by people who paint on cardboard.
It is not to be found in photographs
Or on the postcards people send abroad —
Selfconscious round-mouthed choirs — O, O *Myfanwy*
Or the fat, bleating sheep cascading down
From a green hill into a shepherd's pocket.
You hear it in the valleys, right enough,
And in the hillsides. You should seek it out
In the secluded places where the natives
Drive round in B-reg cars, looking for somewhere
To dump the broken chair, the clapped-out fridge,
The tired Dralon two-point-four piece suite.
Bin-bagged effluvia of valley life
Abandoned. Like unwanted babes in jars
Crying for rescue on the mountainside.
Exposed. Anonymous. The voice of Wales
Sounds like torn plastic caught in old barbed wire:
Black tethered tongues erratically flapping.
The sound of Wales is that of sad hands, clapping.

Rupert

The things that frighten us when young
Are things we're forced to live among

By adults who assume that we
Are shielded by simplicity

From negative extrapolation
Of standard nursery narration.

An unforgiveable mistake.
Myself when young would lie awake

Reiterating what they'd said
Over and over in my head;

Relentless Hudibrastic verse
Laying an intellectual curse

Upon a child who lay in terror
Because of their judgmental error.

I saw it clearly every night
After they took away the light.

It was not tiger, was not shark
That waited in the velvet dark;

Murderous, manic, giggling, dribbling,
A hideous worse-favoured sibling

Of Wendigos and Calibans —
A hairless bear with human hands.

A Cold Night on the Wall

"*Miles Romanus sum; arma virumque cano.*
It's going to be a cold night on the wall —
The sky's too high; there are too many stars
And all my leather gear is damp and dull.
Rufus has ten more minutes. Let him come
And get me when it's time. Let his dog-breath
Crisp on his beard until his watch is up.
I'll stay here in the wash-house underneath
The atrium. There's still a drop of wine
That's bought and paid-for. I shall see it off;
Let Rufus come and get me when it's time.
Bugger Brigantia! I've had enough
Of bloody Celts."

              The fuddle-headed soldier
Pokes with his short-sword at the wash-house floor,
Methodically winkling-out and flicking
The little tesserae: one, two, three, four . . .
Rome was not built in a day: Brutus sits
Meticulously picking it to bits.

Language Difficulty

Welsh is a mad language; there are no words in it.
Not words as Anglo-Saxons understand them.
Definite, finished words that stand for things.
Words purpose-built and unequivocal.
English has words. Ten times as many words
As there are things for them to be names for.
In Welsh it's more a case of things per word;
Pick one from the few in the dictionary —
Pwll: it's "a pit, a pool, a hole, a lake"
And you fight with the Celtic vacillation
Needing to know which, beating your stiff brain
Into a compromise — perhaps *pwll* is the darkness
That is bounded by pitness and lakeness;
Maybe the spirit of the depth itself,
A deep, dark damp, filling an emptiness.

To study Welsh is like embracing Buddhism,
Seeing the world outwith the things in it.
Glas is both "blue" and "green". The Saxon spirit
Howls for a certainty. One or the other!
Who says the two are incompatible?
Certainly not the sea; I asked it once.

Once I worked late into the night, searching
For words that would stand up and take the weight
Of the great sadness that comes to me sometimes,
Into the hole left by the sort of joy
We used to know in childhood — *"Mark my words —
You carry on like that and there'll be tears
Before bedtime."* The hurt of missing something
You never knew you had till it was gone.
Sadness for sadness' sake. Tears on a taut face
Still stretched from too much laughter. Welsh has it;
Simple as stocking-stitch, easy as breathing —
Listen: inhale — *hwyl*; exhale — *hiraeth*.

Ebbw Fach

I think the river is a long brown dog
Sniffing along an unadopted alley,
Jumping the dead brown fox, the flaccid frog —
I think the river is a long brown dog
Engaged in desultory dialogue
With every sunken supermarket trolley
I think the river is a long brown dog
Sniffing along an unadopted alley.

The Painter's Mother

by Lucian Freud

Clothed, defiantly, up to the chin;
The silky tie-necked blouse not disarranged.
Not so much as a button out of true.
But still the face is anxious *"Will he strip me*
Bare as he has dared with his own daughters?
Will he show other people underneath
To hollows and angles that are not his;
The folds of old flesh that he has no right to?

Whatever should I do
If he should dare to break the great taboo
Oedipus lost his eyes for, even with eyes alone
And although the rough touch is just a brush?"
So the old lady's eyes stare from the picture
But do not follow one about the room;
They catch and hold *his* eyes — her son's eyes —
Somewhere between *"please"* and *"don't you dare!"*

But his eyes are elsewhere. On the bamboo
Growing in slender stilts in the great jar
Behind her head. This is the only secret
That he lets slip: there by the grace of God,
Or by human omission, a small, dull
Common-or-garden fern is flourishing
Among the main display. An oversight —
Or then again, perhaps an act of love.

First Love

An evening after school. In uniform.
The classics club had organised a trip
To hear a lecture on *The Odyssey*
By Robert Graves.

I put my name down, not to hear the words
Of a great classics scholar, but the voice
Of the love-poet who had set the first fire
In my small, clean grate.

Oh, he was ordinary; ill-at-ease,
Base needs having brought him there to hold forth
On the minutiae of Nausicaa
And her laundry basket.

He was extraordinary; showed me a man
Naked, in need, stepping into my view
Slime-stained and salt-encrusted from a sea
That had wearied of him.

And I, a princess among sullen schoolgirls
Offered him safety, sought his eyes with mine
So as to spare his shame, calling to him
Down rows of chairs.

White arms, poet? I'll show you white arms.
Slow-rolling the sleeve of a limp school blouse;
A tongue-tip peeping, a stigma, flower-sex,
Flickertouching a moist lip.

But it registered merely as a fidget,
Accelerating his delivery.
Since then I've sometimes tried the same slow trick
With more success.

The Awakening

It was a dream. *I was with Robert Graves*
And had been showing him the way somewhere.
He was in uniform. His sad-dog face
Crowned by a cap that had seen better days.
I had conveyed what he needed to know
And he was easy in his mind. Together
We walked my way for a while before parting
And paused a moment on a massive bridge
Too big for the thin stream dawdling below.
The coping stones were warm from the strong sun
That made soft mustard of his battledress.

We both knew it was time for him to go.
He had an assignation. He was late.
"I'll go" he said "and hope I get a lift" —
He smiled — "and thanks again." I watched him go;
A tall, sure figure clad in yellow dust.

His further safety was within my gift:
From the dark foyer of a small hotel
I called a friend. I said I'd see him right
If he would pick up Robert in his car
With the appearance of coincidence.
That done, I stood holding the telephone,
My cheek and chin feeling warm Bakelite,
My fingers fiddling with the twisted cord
In its twin sleeves of wrinkled stockinette . . .

You broke wind thunderously. The first time
In seven years that you had made so free
With the great space between us. Bright staccato;
A market-trader ripping leathercloth
In fits and starts.

Wide awake in the ensuing silence
I saw you still asleep and understood

That a rare ease coming into your mind
Gave blessing to your body's liberty.

I don't think I have ever loved you more.

Late Submission

An idea for an opening event for the Ebbw Vale Garden Festival

How about this one, then; this one has everything —
A real Welsh focus, lots of local jobs —
It even, in the long term, saves you money.
An all-round winner. This is what you do.
Instead of tarting-up the area
And planting bloody daffodils in rows
All through that little town the Yanks call "Quim";
Instead of pulling down the old Marine
And turning it into a parking space,
Leave it alone until the opening night;
Leave all the loose coal and the winding-gear
And make it look as if it's still a go.
Then, when you get the punters through the gates,
Say your piece, cut the tape — and blow it up!
You'd have to look into the safety thing
Of course. And have a word with Equity.
Nothing the PR people couldn't handle.
An instant pit disaster! Lovely stuff!
The fire department could mount a display —
And what a showcase for the Gwent Police!
You could pay signers-on to limp about
And local women could dress up and weep.
The thing has endless possibilities.
You could sell bits of it as souvenirs
For the duration of the Festival.
Go on. This one's a winner. Ask yourselves:
Who in the great wide world would miss a chance
To watch somebody else's tragedy.

Antony and Cleopatra:

is it Tragedy?

. . . . No. Of the stuff of Tragedy
Nothing remains. A dying lion roars.
An ageing she-cat plays the calling queen.
The ending is begun; the dying fall
Of martial music transcends Tragedy,
Links us with play and players in a small
Exquisite sadness. There, despite the grace
Of God, go most of us . . .

C*it*s I*ter*upt*s

Crosswords in bed. Last night we finished it
In the most satisfying way. Together.
Cries of discovery and delight
As our thought-processes sparked one another
Made little echoes in our duvet-tent.
Clustered together round the anglepoise
Signs of our cruciverbal element —
Two cocoas and a packet of rich teas.
Tonight was cheerless by comparison.
You called a sudden halt to the proceedings.
Said something hurtful, threw the crossword down
And turned your back to me and started reading.
A gust of wind slamming the gates of heaven;
A form of mental torture: 6, 11.

What Janet Said

(in passing, in the newsroom)

"This is for you" says Janet. She extends
her pretty pat-hands, putti-botty pink,
offering me a little tube of cream.

"For your poor hands" she says. "They look so dry.
When I look at your hands, I want to *cwtch** them.
You really should take better care of them;
they're so much *older* than the rest of you."

I look at them. They are big hands, but slim,
and their skin fits them like a wellworn glove.
I'm sure of them. Those hands have done more things
than gentle Janet gives me credit for.

I clench a fist. That fist has clung,
don't-do-or-die, to a door handle
holding at arm's length a wooden shield
from a bad man the worse for one-too-many.

I flutter fingers whose skilled effleurage
has whispered a child to sleep and awoken
the sleepy sex of a reluctant lover,
moving alone like spiders in the dark.

Workaday toolfingers whose busy picking
of noses, guitars, dropped stitches, mortice-locks
and suchlike oakum still daily produces
small results to be relied upon.

Two hands, partners in crime and creation
working together in the frosty dark;
Left sliding deftly into a ewe's womb
drawing a picture of a folded lamb
that Right can understand and act upon,
drawing the actual lamb into reality.
Friends operating independently,
coming together for applause and grief.

I watch two hands on the ugly keyboard
turning themselves to New Technology,
getting to grips with the work in hand —
making paper to wrap fish.

I owe a good friend an apology
because what Janet said is true. My hands
are so much older than the rest of me.

(*Welsh word, means 'cuddle')

Occasional Poem

for Robert Roberts

Caroline felt taken-advantage-of
When someone told her that Auden was gay.
She found the verses she had grown to love
No longer spoke to her in the same way
As when in schoolgirl dreams she'd longed to trace,
From the safe pillow of his faithless arm,
The friendly furrows of his sleeping face.
She felt betrayed, she said, and wished him harm.

I comforted her; said I understood.
We talked of love, and truth and poetry.
She thanked me, saying I had done her good
And that one day she'd do the same for me.

Today I could have put her to the test.
Today you mentioned that Pope was a dwarf
Who wore a complicated canvas vest
So he could stand without folding in half —
A childhood ailment's cruel legacy.
You clearly thought that everybody knew
So I kept *stumm*. But it was news to me;
I looked it up to see if it was true.

It was. It is. And so I had no choice
But to believe. And I felt somehow "had"
Because I had been blinded by the voice
In which he spoke. The supercilious cad.
Erudite Flashman. Darcy's brilliant brother.
I hadn't spotted the deformity;
His verse declared him to be something other —
And then I spotted the enormity
Of where my thoughts were leading: "Had I known
I would have read his verse more tenderly;

24

Added an understanding of my own
To re-interpret his acerbity."

Should poets annotate their poetry,
Append a photograph, declare intention
Lest they fall foul of Caroline, or me —
Uninformed prejudice, or condescension.

The Stainless Child

(For Jane B, who found the concept objectionable)

It's not a blinking, Blake-ish innocence
this stainlessness. It's more the kind of strangeness
that makes your feet uncertain in new shoes.

The first stains are not steps to perdition —
just sad, inevitable interventions,
like the first scratches on anything new.

Think of the patina a chair acquires;
all the character arsekissed into it
by recognition and unthinking use.

This is a chair. Bumshelf — back up, knees bend,
squat, sit on it. That is a child. Show it
and share with it, shaping its adulthood.

It's not a burdensome virginity
waiting like a tin of good salmon; sacred,
unopened till a special guest arrives.

Rather, a swift succession of first times;
genuine never-to-be-repeated offers
of opportunities to observe something,

dragged with the red rags of birth from another place,
a time when you were it, the baby, she —
the stop-frame just before you became Jane.

Semper Hospes

(after Martial)

Answer me this: how come it always works
That every time you come to visit me
I, as your host, must pander to your quirks
To save the face of hospitality,
But when in turn I come to you to visit
You say "please bear in mind you're just a guest;
This is *my* house." That isn't civil is it?
In spite of this I always do my best
To do what is expected, so how come
This paradox: *cur hospes semper sum?*

Looking for Lambs

The townfolk steal it from us, this precious hour;
They insist on their "nice light nights" come what may
As though their annual tinkering with the clock
Somehow lengthens the day.

The townfolk stole it from me, this fine tup lamb.
If I hadn't waited till far too late for the light
That had been here an hour by this time yesterday
The lamb would have been all right.

Damn me for a lousy shepherd. Dark or not
I should have been here an hour or more ago.
I say so, over and over, as though the saying
Could somehow make it so.

The old ewe comes bustling up for a handful of nuts
And I smack her one on the snout and give her a cursing.
If the old waster had only been up to her job
He'd have been up and nursing.

But he came feet-first and drowned in his own juice
Just because she didn't clean him and I wasn't there.
And blaming the absent idiots sops up the anger
So the loss is better to bear.

And year after year the townfolk keep on doing
This wholly illogical, indefensible thing
And calling it Summer Time without understanding
How their Summer steals my Spring.

Sea Cucumbers

In a word, baroque.
A present from God to the new sea.
Artfully contrived by a whimsical Providence
So as to appear spontaneous.
An inventive explosion;
Random excrescences wittily put on
In a bid to try out all the ideas at once.

Glorious one-offs from the age of divine experiment
In new, first-time Plasticine, the colours freshly squeezed,
Not yet degenerated to the nondescript,
The universal grey, the re-worked stuff of elephants.

But the new needs of the land called for mass production
And knife-edge deadlines killed the creative spark
So that later batches were rolled, extruded, machined;
Turned out in quantity to a slimmed-down specification.

Slick. Standard. Ubiquitous.
Just slugs.

The Leprechaun Dances

The Pure Drop, Listowel, 19.5.96

There's a knowing look on the face of the woman
With the big blonde hair and the opulent bosom
As she reaches deep in the recessed cleft
And flips her tits to right and left
In the swift deft fishing for a silver string
Whence dangles an amulet, a pretty little thing
In the shape of a perfect, tiny man.

> *"I am a man of Ireland*
> *Of the holy land of Ireland:*
> *You sir, whosoe'er ye be*
> *If ye've an ounce of charity*
> *I pray to God ye'll dance with me*
> *In Ireland."*

She draws him forth from her deep dark place
And she wipes the fluff off his fierce little face.
He has eyes all lined from winking and grinning,
A head like a hazelnut, black hair thinning,
And a serge suit shining at the pressure points.
Then, whipping the linchpins out of his joints
She sets him dancing on the polished floor.

> *"I am a man of Ireland*
> *Of the holy land of Ireland:*
> *You sir, whosoe'er ye be*
> *If ye've an ounce of charity*
> *I pray to God ye'll dance with me*
> *In Ireland."*

Like the ring of a hammer on my hard heart's door
Is the knocking of his hard little shoes on the floor

And high in the air he twists and prances
While my stomach plummets and my hard heart dances
And the taut serge shines on his dear little bum
As it hovers out of reach like a shrink-wrapped plum
And the loose change jiggles in his pocket.

> *"I am a man of Ireland*
> *Of the holy land of Ireland:*
> *You sir, whosoe'er ye be*
> *If ye've an ounce of charity*
> *I pray to God ye'll dance with me*
> *In Ireland."*

And now in the night when sleep comes hard
And the old dog howls in the empty yard
I can hear the sound of the dancing man
Like an old tin whistle or a sad bodhran
And I make him a promise that as soon as may be
I will go to Listowel and I'll set him free
And I'll wind him up and he'll dance for me
For I've seen the place where he keeps his key . . .

. . . . . . *And I'll remember it as long as I live!*

Villanelle for Two Friends

The nicest people seem to come in pairs
And it's a double blessing when they do —
A comely coupledom, with no false airs.

A private peace peculiarly theirs
But which rubs off on other people, too.
The nicest people seem to come in pairs.

A sort of self-sufficiency that shares
Its comfort without even trying to.
A comely coupledom, with no false airs;

In ordinary day-to-day affairs
Each bears in mind the other's point of view.
The nicest people seem to come in pairs;

An arithmetic paradox, which squares
Their simple sum, creating something new —
A comely coupledom with no false airs.

Two people effortlessly holding shares
In one another, like the two of you.
The nicest people seem to come in pairs,
A comely coupledom, with no false airs.

Small Farm at the Edge of Town

1. THE ELECTRIC SHEPHERD

I love the sounds of the place, but the noise spoils it.
The racket of geese let loose in the early morning,
The mouth-full call of a ewe through chewed grass,
Pigeons clattering up or muttering down,
The inelegant digestion of horses;
Even the workshop babel of hammer and adjective,
The unholy clamour of St Teilo's bells,
The rhythmic soughing of the occasional train —
These are safe sounds, expected and acceptable.
The noise is something altogether different.

It is the thrumming of the town's lifeblood pumping
From a heart too horrible to keep in its soft body.

Substation. Centre point of a singing web
Holding the whole farm gullivered to the ground
By a constant, whispered 50-cycle threat.
Pylons stand over the stock like blinded giants
Groping for any interloper in their purlieu.
Low cloud makes crik-crak demons spit between their fingers,
Mocking the moaning of days that have lost their nights.

Security lights — clap, plap, flip, plop —
Chuck sudden fistfuls of brightness at windblown trees
Spotlighting saleable moveables in the yard.
Even in the slow fields where things are not so critical
Light spills like fruit from an overturned barrow:
Orange from the estate, peach from the main road,
Lime and loganberry from the level crossing,
All liquidised into a sticky, creeping glow.

Alone, awake, I hang like the Cumæan Sybil
Dangling in the doorway between day and night
Longing for proper darkness, real silence.

2. MENDING HEDGE

Fingers never forget the feel of baler band
Nor palms the cut of it as you pull it tight;
Twice round the stake, once round the hurdle,
Half-hitch — to acknowledge a temporary job,
A resolve to do it again, better, later.

One instruction on the list of things to do
Was to put the draft ewes on a fresh pasture
After checking the hedge for gaps and attending
To any dangerous ones that I came across.

Oh how it all came back. The bitter smell of the iron
As I threw the crowbar, spearing the soft earth.
Slide of the stake between my hands as I hefted it;
Thump of the hammer, throb of the haft, as I hit it.

Gently at first, staccato, one-two-three-four.
Then, when I felt it bite deep and settle in
I gave it all I had, balancing heronwise,
Bracing it upright with the weight of my left foot.

Two stakes, one hurdle tied in place with band.
The sort of running repair I did in the old days
When such things were tests to be judged by critical neighbours
And the sheep on the other side of the gap were mine.

As I stepped back a thorn caught and I heard on the wind
What was once the dearest voice in all the world.
Felix. My mentor, master, lover, friend, paying
A Yorkshire compliment "Aye. A good job, and cheap."

3. SOLSTICE

In the field below the farm schoolboys were drinking lager,
Long legs stretched out on the short brown grass,
Tossing sexual epithets back and forth
Like rude tennis: *fuck — cunt — fuck — advantage Kevin.*

I had seen lambs running in a crazy bunch
So I ran too, guessing under my breath — bad dogs? rough boys?
But there was nothing, only the ewes' querulous bleating
As their lambs ran amok in the last gasp afternoon.

And as I watched, more and more of the lambs joined in.
Tiny ones, potbellied, bouncing on skinny legs
Made a picot edge to the shifting woollen knot
That had formed around two boisterous baby rams.

How the young tups squared up to one another!
These lowland lambs would never grow real rams' weaponry;
Even the bony ridges of their brows were padded
With deep round teddy-quiffs of curly wool.
But they fought anyway, drawing back, advancing, rearing,
Colliding knobby skulls with soft, dull thumps.

Sounds of combat rang loud in the languid air:
Fuck — cunt — thump. Shit — thump — fuck.
Until both teams called quits.

In the night the world turned and began going backwards.
In the morning a man gathered lager cans into a sack
While I counted ruminating mashed-potato sheep, dozing
In dollops under the hedge.

Scantlings

Passing through roadworks on an autumn morning
We could not help but notice the lack of action.
The great machines lay idle among the workmen
Not one of whom was actually working.

They looked busy, though. Pursing their lips and frowning
And not quite meeting the eyes of the passing traffic.
You quoted Pepys — *"waiting for scantlings, sir"* —
And we winked and tapped our noses at each other.

Scantling. A silly word however you mean it.
A critical measurement, a miserly smidgen,
An insignificant fillet or batten of wood.
A word you might go a lifetime without a need for.

On a train alone, less than a day later
I pecked with a pen at a crossword, missing you,
When there it was, staring at me. Sixteen down — *scantling* —
And the fun and the fear of the random struck me again.

They happen so often, these surreptitious twinnings,
As if somebody somewhere were playing at Pelmanism,
Turning things over to match them with one another,
Fiddling with scantlings lest they forget Leviathan.

So they are not cracks in the Order, but underpinnings;
Quick glimpses of the free ends of the mythical strings
Stitched out of sight under all that loose, cold skin
Trussing the flaccid carcase of the universe.

A Poem in Praise of the 1995 Second Class Christmas Stamp

The Royal Mail have done it!
Away with bells and elves!
They've found the perfect picture
To symbolise themselves.

A jolly little robin
With frosty beak and feet
A-peeping from a postbox —
Aaaah! — doesn't it look sweet!

It flashes forth the scarlet front
We know and trust the most;
And then it lifts its little tail
And shits upon our post.

Last Love

Time was when I saw us tall;
Mountaintop lovers casting one long twined shadow,
Having dominion over a stretching sea.
But we grow old together and the vision shrinks
Till we are tiny figures, separate,
Adrift in a choppy river side by side
In a pair of walnut shells.

And in the times when either one of us
Slips into one of those swift bits
Where you go fast and nowhere
But round and round and round,
The other clutches overhanging things,
Holds on. And waits.

The Iron Horse

Mike made the iron horse in a spare moment.
He was the second son of a hill farmer
With no chance of taking over the farm,
And so he learned a blacksmith's skills instead.

A blacksmith's work is not what it once was.
He was an agricultural engineer.
He mended other people's implements
And redesigned them when they broke too often.

He made the iron horse in a spare moment
Out of the same things his life was made of.
He welded it together; nuts, bolts, swarf
Rearing to strike the air with two bent nails.

I saw it dancing up on a high shelf
And loved it. I said it was beautiful,
Which he gruffly denied. I tried to buy it.
"Tek it" he said. "It's neither nowt nor summat."

I took it then, treasure it now because
When I next visited his dirty workshop
I noticed he had made another moment
To make himself another iron horse.

Change of Heart

My true love hath my heart, and I have his.
At first they said that this "could not be done",
Then "public funds should not be used for this";
We fought them in the civil courts and won.
They had a bit of trouble with the pipes —
He's AC/DC with a left-hand thread
And our connections aren't the standard types —
But he's got mine and I've got his instead.
At first our mutual joy was unconfined
But I am troubled with a growing fear.
I am no longer easy in my mind.
I feel that this was not a good idea.
I'd say so, but the bugger of it is
My true love hath my heart — and I've got his.

Unplasticised Polyvinyl Chloride

> *Artex, when it is wet, smells of corruption;*
> *Dry, it forms into a ponderous scab.*
> *All its aspects follow the same soddit course*
> *As Nature making the best of a bad job.*

Turning and turning in the widening gyre
The hawk no longer hears the pargeter;
Only the wet hiss of the plastic comb
Across the surfaces laid down by men
Who have forgotten, or who never had
The skill to float them flat.

> *Who will buy my luscious conservatories?*
> Fresh picked-up this morning from the factory
> Flat packed and ready to assemble;
> Come buy, come buy.

> *Who will buy my sweet sealed units?*
> Tilt and turn and tight as a virgin.
> Keep all that precious heat inside your house
> Till the walls weep for joy.

> *Who will buy my fine new fascias?*
> Choice, all choice, a choice of white or woodlook
> With no unsightly knots or wicked splinters,
> No smell of sawn grain.

> *Who will buy casements, light as a feather?*
> Cheap plastic eyes for your windowless soul,
> Never need painting, last for a lifetime
> (Never ask me whose).

Oh. . . . .*The fair maid of Mornington, to market she did step*
And on her way did chance to meet a Home Improvements rep.
He flattered her and flannelled her and promised joys galore

If she would but permit him to refurbish her front door.
'Twas straightway accomplished with a wham-bam-slam
And he left in a hurry with a "thank you ma'am"
And a promise of forever and a false address
And nine months later she was in a sorry mess.
Her hinges settled and her door didn't fit
But she couldn't whip a sliver off the side of it.
She couldn't fit a catflap; her pussy went thin.
Her storm-sill buckled and the water trickled in.
Her house was ruined and her heart was sore
And she longed in vain for her old front door.

                                    . . . . .Trad.

In days to come social historians
And students of vernacular architecture
Will spot the tendencies we overlook,
Being party to them. They will appreciate
How uPVC follows sudden money
And feeds on it.

Redundancy payments are like fairy gold,
Turning too easily into dead leaves.
Inflation sucks them thin like a boiled sweet.
Idleness breaks out in a rash of small needs.
Depreciation drips, like water on limestone,
On cars and furniture; moth and rust doth consume.
To people grieving for yesterday, fearing tomorrow,
It is easy to sell the concept of Forever.

                    What price Forever, anyway?
                    It seems that we are still not quite at ease
                    With the fact of our own being demonstrably
                    Biodegradable over the medium term.
                    Slowly we lower our sights. Now we demand
                    Not that our buildings outlast us as monuments
                    To our own lives and the greater glory of God,
                    But that they see
                    Us
                    Out.

(From) *The Suitors*

To-day we have sniffing of parts. Yesterday
We had increased awareness. And to-morrow —
If we are not extremely vigilant —
We shall have misalliance. The lurcher is in heat.
Outside, the visitors, eager to oblige.
      And to-day we have sniffing of parts.

SLY, WHO IS NOT IN THE RUNNING

Away in the west lives mighty Sly
With his peasant's thews and his poet's eye;
He has dinosaur ribs, he has coconut hair
And the spindly legs of a Mackintosh chair.

Sly is a long-dog, thin as a rail
With umbrella feet and a shoestring tail.
His bodily wind has the pungent smell
Of the breeze that blows from the jaws of hell.

He is lightning when putting himself to his speed,
Though it's not very often he sees the need.
His actions are few but his thoughts run deep;
A philosopher-dog who needs his sleep.

He sleeps in a heap from morn till night
Like a dead dog dropped from a dizzying height,
Rising and falling like dough in a draught
With occasional mutterings fore and aft.

His ears are deaf and his eyes are blind
And the itch for a bitch never crosses his mind.
This is the way he was born to lie —
Slothful, somnolent, celibate Sly.

BIG BILL, THE BUTCHER'S DOG

He's one of the worst;
He always knows first
When a bitch is coming in season,
But he acts *distrait*
As though coming this way
For no particular reason.
He thinks he's God's gift
And his leg he will lift
By way of a friendly greeting
Then he'll piddle and spray
In a haphazard way
To hint at his hope of a meeting.
He leaves small pools
And curlicue stools
In the hope of gaining her favour
But she isn't for him
So she covers her quim
With the tail that the good Lord gave her.

JESS, THE JOLLY MONGREL

Here's Jess, the jolly mongrel.
He passes twice a day.
Then stands about and sniffs the wind
A little way away.
He knows I know he's out there
He knows his cause is lost
But he hangs around for ages with
His furry fingers crossed.
His head is like a bottle-brush
His tail a runner bean
And a body like a bolster fills
The distance in between.
He has nothing much to offer her
Except his hybrid vigour

But he loiters on the corner and
He clearly seems to figure,
Since he himself has come about
Through someone's carelessness,
The laws of chance might smile upon
The jolly mongrel Jess.

SNIFFER, THE QUESTING BEAST

Behold, the beast the neighbours roar at
Semper quaerens quod devorat
Prising up the lids of bins,
Making off with empty tins,
Crusts and crumbs of pies and pasties,
Dirty nappies, ladies' nasties,
Skins and bones and shucks and shells —
Anything that drips or smells
He'll take away and either eat
Or lick and leave along the street
Transferring things that they had hidden
From private bin to public midden
Exposing thus their secret mess
In all its rank unloveliness.
They rate him *non persona grata*
And stone him like a Christian martyr.

He leaves his card but does not press
His suit upon the fair princess.
He finds a sunny spot instead;
He lifts his leg, he bends his head
Then slowly, singlemindedly,
Commits *fellatio-de-se*.

MINOS, THE BULL TERRIER

When first observed his looks suggest a failure
Either of manufacture or design.
His barrel chest and giant genitalia
Require his legs to be tacked to his spine
And bent like felloes in a wheelwright's yard
Around these overstated attributes.
His general demeanor is rock hard;
He has the air of being in cahoots
With forces of malevolence and death.
His fat face forms a vaguely vapid grin
But it was put there so he can draw breath
While grabbing gobfuls of his canine kin.
Once having taken hold he won't let go.
One wonders why the good Lord made him so.

PREM, THE PARIAH DOG

"Little black dog from the takeaway. Never trust him.
He has the eyes of a lascar, they've probably seen things
Better not spoken-of. He has been to places
That might have rubbed off on him. Don't touch.
Who knows what manner of rubbish they feed him;
Even his shit smells different from proper dogshit.
Who told him he could come calling on a white lurcher?
Nobody called him; nobody asked him to come;
He is not welcome here."

But his brown eyes sing of all the hurts you have done him
And the sun makes him smell of oiled hair. Spikenard and Myrrh.
His eyes hold secrets that he might trade for pleasure.
Here, Prem, I will stroke your black fur;
Come, I will introduce you to Penelope.
Here, Prem, come. Don't look at me like that.
Oh, Prem — come back. Why did you run away?

SHINTO, THE JAPANESE CHIN

Tiny dog pauses
sniffs invisible lotus
piddles a dewdrop

ROBBIE, THE CAIRN TERRIER

O wha will gie the quine her pleasure
O wha will gie't in fullest measure
O wha will gie her weans tae treasure
The rantin dog the daddie o'em

O wha will gie 'em een sae beady
O wha will mak 'em plump an' greedy
O wha will niver see 'em needy
The rantin dog the daddie o'em

O wha will tak the weans aboot
O wha will show 'em whaur tae root
O wha will teach 'em when tae scoot
The rantin dog the daddie o'em.

PENELOPE REPLIES:

Oh, devious dog, you've had your day;
I don't believe a word you say,
For when you'd had your wicked way
Who'd really tend them day-to-day —
And who would whelp them anyway?
Your plans, I fear, have gang'd agley
For *I* will choose the daddy o'em!

Talkin' Blues

This is the day when I go into town,
And I fold my face in a serious frown
And I hunch my shoulders and I watch my feet
As they take me down into Worcester Street
With my ES40 in my second-best bag,
Polishing the pavement with a long, slow drag
And a sudden little shuffle as I miss the cracks
But it don't work magic 'cos you can't change facts —

I got the deadbeat, downbeat, must-do-better, unemployment blues

Oh, I did the bit with the speculative letters
To a long long list of my elders and betters
And I told them who and I told them why
And most of the buggers didn't bother to reply.
But I do get a job every once in a way
And I get a lot of money for the odd half day
Which I try to declare with a modicum of grace
But the whole damn system blows up in my face.
I told them I worked for the BEEB, which I did;
I read for half a minute and they gave me fifty quid.
The girl pressed the button but it didn't compute —
So little time yielding so much loot.
I suppose, I, too, would think it was a sin
If it happened more often than a lottery win.
And the girls on the counter can't be shouted at
'Cos the fault's in the System and you can't kick that.

I got the deadbeat, downbeat, must-do-better, unemployment blues

Well, I do have a problem with my attitude
But I don't turn nasty and I don't get rude;
I am well aware that it can't be enjoyable
To have to find jobs for the unemployable.
I can't weld circuits and I can't sew bras

I can't colour hair and I can't drive cars.
But I got a letter the other day
To go for an interview at UEA;
I felt my heart do a double-back-flip —
I'd been shortlisted for a Fellowship!
I gave it my best but it all went flat;
They preferred Peter Reading, so that was that.
I tried not to take it as a verdict on my art
But it pricked my pride and it hurt my heart
Though it wouldn't have made me quite so dejected
To lose a job to a guy I respected
If I hadn't been aware that the price of defeat
Was going cap-in-hand back to Worcester Street.

I got the deadbeat, downbeat, must-do-better, unemployment blues

Self-Portrait

In reply to a request for a photograph to accompany a poem

Why should anyone seek pictures of poets?

I do not choose to exist as a fixed picture
Inevitably given the lie to later,
Regretted, superseded, taken down
Leaving only a clean patch on the wall.

I should prefer to hang
Not in your mind's gallery but its concert-hall.
I would rather think of you
Taking me home with you, busy in your head.
Playing me daily gaily in the garden,
Humming me happily about your business.

What I am is whatever you see when you hear me.
Whistle me thoughtfully from time to time —
Allegro, ma non troppo vivace.

(From) A SPELL IN HOSPITAL

For "Tom"
Forsan et haec olim meminisse iuvabit
Virgil; *Aeneid i.203*

Smell 1

As the illness progressed an odour came.
I noticed it first when you weren't there.

Spilled milk and candlegrease. Old kitchen smells
From long ago.

And something else that I had almost forgotten;
The smell that hangs in the air on the cusp
Between love and responsibility.
Memories of the washday awfulness
Of sorting through crispfronted cardigans
And clammy bibs. I lifted your pillow
And held it to me, nosing into the creases;
Far past the age of childbearing, I lay again
Sniffing up all the loathly loveliness
Of the possetty neck-sweat of babies.

Feeding Charybdis

Today we are going to the hospital
To hear results and learn what must be done.
You had the first bath, which is only right,
Yours being the body under consideration,
And there was not much water left for me.

I have washed myself quickly. Now I kneel
Like a colossus over the plughole
Watching the baby maelstrom swallowing
All the small bits of human detritus
Dithering into its tiny bailiwick.

First each coy dancer circles round the spot.
Then comes a mad dive round and round and down
And the wild spin into oblivion.

Now, as the water cools around my thighs,
I search out little bits of you and me.
Small platelets of exfoliated skin,
Gobbets of navel-fluff and pubic hair,
Pushing them forward with a soapy finger
Through the tense surface towards Charybdis.

Dearest, we need all the help we can get
So I am seeking out all sources of power
And offering-up. Always offering-up.

Team Nursing

Watch the nurses playing the talking game.
See them taking the field in twos and threes,
Teams within teams, blue, red, yellow and green
Or any combination of them all.

The game is played with words.
Small, hard ones are tossed deftly back and forth
Between team members. Swift back-passes;
The quickness of the hand deceives the eye,
The whizzing gist all but invisible
To any but the trained initiate.

To patient bystanders they condescend
Carefully, lobbing them low, easy catches
Like adults playing with hamfisted children,
Letting them win by not overtaxing
Their powers of co-ordination:
How are you today, Tom? All right, is it?
The volume pitched louder than necessary,
The enunciation slow and clear.
Eyebrows go up, lips part and the face waits
(Got it, Tom? Good — now throw it back to me.)

It bothers me. How can I let them know
You have been playing this game all your life,
Even acquired a little expertise,
Without being so crass as to expose
My own black belt?

Permanent Rose

While you kept your appointment in theatre
I went to town seeking permanent rose
To keep a promise.

The only shade of watercolour missing
From your collection. You had to have it;
I had to get it for you, and I did.

But when I had paid for the tiny tube
It didn't seem enough. In the posh florist's
I bought a fistful of pink silk roses
And taped the tube under one of the leaves.

They gave me a card and I wrote on it
"Permanent Rose" and one of my cross-kisses,
Trying a little too hard not to ponder
Upon the impermanence of roses
Or on my true love facing the unknown
Without the right shoes or the proper hat.

Awaiting the Return of the Italian Surgeon

We have to trust him, *il piccolo dottore*.
Rested from his *vacanza in Italia*.
We must pray that his stay was in the bosom of his family;
That their love has kept him in touch with the skills of his people —
The fine judgement of his brother Bartolomeo
Whose vineyards are justly famed for their fine Chianti;
The keen eye of his other brother Vittorio
A single still from whose movies makes strong men weep;
The skill with the needle shown by his cousin Gianni
Whose gowns are so much a part of *La Bella Figura*.
But, above all, the decisive touch of *la sua madre*,
Piling the pasta skilfully onto his plate,
Letting it drop artlessly between two forks;
This skill he will apply, *Deo volente*, when faced
With all the great commotion of your guts
Writhing and fainting in coils.

The Bargee

Some members of staff have more regard than others
To what the textbooks call "patient dignity"
But in the course of necessary care,
Of dressing wounds, of changing bedlinen,
There grows a pact between patients and nurses,
A sort of trust, a kind of understanding
That makes dependent nudity acceptable.

The little grey-clad clerk flits like a blowfly
In fits and starts along the corridor,
Twitching the curtains of the side-ward windows
Looking for situations upon which to impinge.
"Oh, Staff . . ." "Oh, Sister . . ." poking her head inside
Insinuating her body in behind it,
Working herself artfully into the best place
For an uninterrupted view.

The only time I ever saw your hand
Move to restore your body's privacy
Was when this nasty little pest barged in
And hovered with administrative questions.
She saw, she knew; and actually bent over
Miming "Oh, dear" and vocalising "sorreeeeee"
Before withdrawing backwards, sucking the last vista
Into her sad and sickly little eyes.

The nurse bent to your dressing
But you were ill at ease. The trust had gone.

Bargee. I wish her ignominy. May she find herself
Summarily compromised in a public place;
Exposed mid-piddle by the freak malfunction
Of an automated toilet; naked in Tesco.

A Little Bell

A little bell, a little golden bell
A little golden Christmas-looking bell
With Santa on his sleigh, waving goodwill
While six wild reindeer rear into the sky
Making a cunning little handle.

If you take it between finger and thumb
And give it the teeniest shake, it tinkles
Like babies' laughter. Such a pretty thing
And it is all for you. Nurse gave it to you
To keep for as long as you need it.

Nurse gave the bell to you because last night
You had a paroxysm of vomiting
That made green curtains run down all four walls
And rang the "help me" bell and no-one came
Because the bell was broken.

So you cried out at the top of your voice
Begging for someone, anyone, to come;
But cries of distress on the ward at night
Are constant and for the most part ignored.
You lay ill and afraid alone.

Today I asked if something could be done
And they brought you the little golden bell.
I went back home and fetched a sleeping bag.
I will be here tonight and every night.
Because I don't believe in Santa Claus.

Bacchanal

Sing, sing the staphylococcus
Lewd entertainer at the court of Bacchus

He's a hunchbacked dwarf with a dumpy shape
That mocks the model of the sacred grape

He follows his master at a limping trot
Disseminating the ignoble rot

He sticks to the rosy fingers of the dawn
When she touches her lips in a decorous yawn

He rides on the eagle to the prize it's found
And he licks round the edges of Prometheus' wound

He nests in the nostrils of the Queen of Troy
And he lurks round the anus of the altar-boy

Sing, sing the staphylococcus
Lewd entertainer at the court of Bacchus

But you, my love, may safely doze;
You can scratch your arse, you can pick your nose.
You'll be safe, my darling, whatever you do —
There's a poet in the corner, so he won't get you.

Open Wound

"That which I most feared has come to pass"

"Get out of your bed" said the Physio.
"Already you're over the worst;
"On your feet and be off —
"Have a jolly good cough —
"Don't worry, your stitches won't burst!"

"I want you to walk" said the Doctor.
"It's vital you do as you're told;
"On your feet. Be a man.
"Do as much as you can —
"Don't worry, your stitches will hold!"

But the thought of the wound bursting open
And spilling your guts on the floor
Was a deep-seated dread
Firmly fixed in your head
That you don't have to face any more.

For the worst that could happen has happened
And the wound is a gargoyle that gapes
With a permanent drip
On its quivering lip
From which bodily fluid escapes.

On a crag within sight of Olympus
Stretched out at the whim of the Fates
Trussed with tubing and wires
Lies the lighter of fires,
Prometheus. Prometheus waits.

Smell 2

The stink of Scutari hangs in the still air
And rises as you shift your thighs in sleep.
You have been dealt too many wounds, my love,
And they are weeping in the dark.

This is the odour of the aftermath
Of any one of a thousand battles
And in the low hours of the early morning
It smells a little too much of defeat.

Kangaroo

Your feeding pump is called a Kangaroo.
All night it eases food into your stomach
Through a thin tube that inhabits your nose.
More plugs, more wires, and a ratchetty wheel
That turns and squeezes every thirty seconds.

In the long, half-awake hospital dreams
I change places with the other kangaroo.
Settling beside you on my heavy haunches
I lift you carefully with unwieldy paws
And fold you, tiny and soft, into my pocket.
Down there in the fluff, among the sweetpapers
Is a secret nipple, source of nourishment
And healing. All night long I nurse you there,
My little secret Joey, in the dark,
In the safe, in the warm, next to my heart.

Aubade

Just as the cock crows in the real world
To wake it to the possibility
Of birdsong, hospital catches its breath
At the first plastic tumbler of the day
Hitting the deck and rattling at random
To a grudging standstill; then exhales
In a state of knowing anticipation
As the same sounds give rise to one another
In an unvarying chronology.
Early risers wheeling their saline drips
Like shopping trolleys to the lavatory.
Bedlam cries of the confused elderly
Tonelessly calling out to dead parents
And wailing at their failure to reply.
Brisk nurses tipping shovelfuls of pills
Like washers into blind men's begging bowls
Until persuasive traders ply their wares
Along the corridor — *Porridge or cornflakes?*
And the first blessed cup of horse-piss tea.

Schindler's Lifts

Hospital is a gamble, so
It's probably as well to know
Exactly where the power lies
That chooses if one lives or dies.
One's tempted to attribute clout
To doctors drifting in and out
Or nurses in relentless shifts:
These are delusions; it's the lifts.

Night and day they come and go
Ferrying people to and fro
Between floors where they want to be
And levels of reality.

You need a lift? You press a tit
Then hum and walk about a bit
And if it seems to take too long
You idly wonder what's gone wrong
But when one comes you soon forget
Your vague unease — and in you get,
Accepting any one of three
With perfect equanimity.

Nobody chooses which will come
In answer to their thrusting thumb
But all the best and all the worst
Stems from which one answers first,
With all eventual rewards
Determined by two motherboards
Designed to operate in tandem —
One rigidly prescribed, one random.

Appealing to authority
Will not subvert their potency;
They are a team — there is no boss:
Clotho, Lachesis, Atropos.